WHAT GOD IS LIKE

by

James Dillet Freeman

NITY BOOKS
UNITY VILLAGE, MISSOURI

CONTENTS

PHOTOGRAPHY: Canadian Government Travel Bureau—p. 25;
Grant Heilman—p. 50; Ted Laatsch—p. 56;
Tony LaTona—pp. 20, 26, 65; Luoma Photos—p. 76;
Roger L. Meisenbach—Cover, pp. 12, 58, 72, 75, 87;
Sy Miller—p. 43; Edward Quigley—p. 66;
H. Armstrong Roberts—pp. 10, 16, 31, 99, 104, 105, 114;
Swiss National Tourist Office—p. 92

PREFACE

When I was making a talk in Amarillo, Texas, a man showed me a letter. The woman who had written it had come to him a few days before. A doctor had just told her that her husband had an inoperable brain tumor and there was no hope. She would be left with two small children to support. The man who gave me the letter said, "I did not know what to say to her, but I happened to have a *Daily Word* on my desk. I gave her that." Now he had received this letter. In it she told how she was finding courage. What had helped her most, she said, was the poem on the back cover of *Daily Word.* She even quoted from it. The poem was one about a laughing mountain (it is in this book).

A woman I met in Birmingham, Alabama, told me a story about another poem, one I had written about imagining violets. (It too is in the book.) "It had meant a lot to me when I first read it," she said, "so I kept it. One day I came home to discover that a neighbor had just lost her husband in an accident. They were dear friends and immediately I thought, 'Oh, I must go to her.' But then I thought, 'What can I say?' I could think of nothing else but your poem about violets. I took it out of the desk where I kept it and started across the yard to her house. This was in January. As I hurried along, I stumbled over something on the lawn. I looked down, and there was a small clump of violets in bloom! Violets don't bloom in Birmingham in January any more than they do in Kansas City in March. But there they were. I went in, and put that little clump of violets and your poem into her hand."

I am not sure how a laughing mountain or those imagined violets said what needed to be said to help two women at a critical moment of their lives.

And don't turn to the poems in the thought that you can figure out what it was they said to the women. I doubt if you can.

Often people tell me what certain poems say to them. Sometimes I get the poems out and read them to see if I can figure out how they meant that to those readers, but I hardly ever can.

But that is the very nature of poetry. What does a poem say? It says what it says to you!

Many of the poems in this book I wrote for *Daily Word*. The editor showed me a picture she wanted to use on the cover and asked me if I could write a poem about it.

I always say, "Yes." I am afraid to tell her, "No." She might ask somebody else and find out they could do it, too.

The editor is too wise to ask me what the poem is going to say. She knows I will not know until I have written it. Often I am as surprised as anybody.

When people ask me what a poem says, I can only tell them to read the poem. That is what I have to do.

The poem said to me what I wrote down. If I could have said it better, I would have written that.

A poem however is hardly ever obvious. A laughing mountain may say courage and imagined violets may say peace and strength.

I may think I am writing about Christmas or bread or lilacs or bridges—and all the time I am really writing about life or about you or about me, only what I am saying cannot be effectively said in a more direct or abstract way.

This is why poetry is an ideal form of communication when one is trying to write about God, as I am in this book. This is why the Bible and most of the great scriptures of the world are mainly poetic. The Hindus say that all one can say about God is, "He is." But a poem does not try to say what He is; instead it lets you feel what He is like.

What then should my book of poems do for you?

First of all, it should sing for you, and it should set you singing. Poetry is song. The whole universe moves in rhythm; our pulse dances, keeping time to the music of our central being. Let us give it tunes then to which it may dance in joy.

Also, I trust my poems will breathe courage. May a line here and there flash in your imagination like a spark and catch fire to your thoughts—to warm your heart for a passing moment, or perhaps to light a light in you that will cast a brightening ray down all the long path of your life.

Above all, I hope my poems will help you to keep a sense of wonder, which is the ability to be perpetually surprised by the freshness of things. Without this, life runs down and turns into a daily dull repetition and humdrum succession of events.

When you put down my book, whether you have read one poem or a hundred, I pray that you may always have a new sense of the wonder of God, a sense that you live in a world of wonders, and a sense that not the least of wonders is yourself.

WHAT GOD IS LIKE

I did not know what God is like
Until a friendly word
Came to me in an hour of need—
And it was God I heard.

I did not know what God is like
Until I heard love's feet
On errands of God's mercy
Go up and down life's street.

I did not know what God is like
Until I felt a hand
Clasp mine and lift me when alone
I had no strength to stand.

I think I know what God is like,
For I have seen the face
Of God's son looking at me
From all the human race.

THE TRIPLE ROSE

I saw upon one stem
Three roses, and in them
Could of a sudden see
God in His Trinity.

For one rose is my flesh:
Here in this fair rose-mesh
Of sense and sight and sound
Life is enthroned and crowned.

And one rose is my mind:
Out of the undefined
And formless light of thought,
Eternal Truth is wrought.

And one rose is my heart:
I know that I am part
Of God, being capable of
The selflessness of love.

I saw upon one stem
Three roses, and in them
Could of a sudden see
God's triple rose in me.

HAD WE THE EYES

How fair a world
Around us lies,
Heaven unfurled
Had we the eyes

To see the worth
Of all that is.
Like heaven earth
Is also His.

How can the rose
More than the clod
From which it grows
Embody God?

THE FINEST FLOWERING

God is a kind of seed.
To grow He does not need
A sage, or saint, or priest,
But in one of the least,
Where there has been no sign
Of anything divine,
Without forewarning He
May of a sudden be!
The flower of God may start
In any human heart
And it will leave no room
For any other bloom.

O HAPPY MYSTERY

I note with solemn awe
The world is run by law
And I must try to learn
The rules on which things turn.
But law, if law makes sense,
Implies intelligence,
Which means that the unknown
Must be mind like my own,
And if that's true I stand
In no uncaring hand.
And so I sense above
Even God's law, God's love,
O happy mystery,
A heart that beats for me!

LOVE'S PURPLE PATCHES

I think that God is love because
He makes things lovelier than laws
Call for God slips into the batches
Of life's gray paint love's purple patches:
Sunsets, bluebirds, butterflies,
Rainbows in rain—God likes surprise.
Take lilacs—just the leaves would be
A heart-shaped miracle to see;
But God adds flowers in spring, a foam
Of purple bees on a honeycomb,
A violet swarm of stars that cling
In galaxies of glittering;
And lilacs are not leaf and bloom,
But utter attar, sheer perfume,
Fragrance! Lilacs tell me love
Is what things are constructed of.
I note how God has wrapped this globe
In lilac air like a seamless robe.
And I sense, no less than lilacs, you
And I, at heart, are love's stuff, too.

O LOVE, THE LOVELIEST NAME

He who was love incarnate came
Saying, "Love one another." All
His teaching sums up in love's name.
Lord Love, upon your name I call;
Your name above all names I laud,
O Love, the loveliest name of God!

In this one name the music of
Man's fairest longings is outpoured,
For love is God and God is love:
Love, I will have you for my lord;
Your name above all names I laud,
O Love, the loveliest name of God!

And I will do your perfect will
And I will know your name by heart,
For I will say it over till
I fix it in my inmost part;
Your name above all names I laud,
O Love, the loveliest name of God!

GOD IS IN THE MIDST OF ME!

Where is God? Is He afar,
Out beyond the farthest star?
No, He is not far but near;
He is nearer than my fear,
He is nearer than my need.
When I call Him He will heed;
He is in the midst of me!

When the way uncertain is,
He will hold my hand in His;
In the valley of the night
I will have an inward light.
He is faith—I will not fear;
He is love, and He will hear;
He is in the midst of me!

Need I even call at all?
Knows He not each sparrow's fall?
Lord Immanuel, Thou art
Ever present in my heart,
And however far I roam
In Thy heart I am at home;
Thou art in the midst of me!

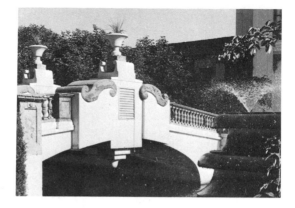

CHRIST IS THE BRIDGE

Christ is the bridge on which we cross
Out of our soul's apartedness;
Christ is the cross by which we bridge
Our gulf of empty-heartedness.

"He who has seen me has seen God,"
He said to us, "I am your brother.
As I am one with God and you,
You are all one with one another."

Christ is the human form of truth
We are divinely fashioned of,
And when we asked, "What is Your name?"
He said to us, "My name is love."

BREAD

In every bit of bread I break,
I see Christ's body given for all;
For nothing is so plain and small
But in its essence must partake
Of Him. All hearts are holy ground;
Could I but draw the veils apart,
I should see in the humblest heart
God's Son enthroned and crowned.
Why do I seek, lo, here! lo, there!
And wonder why He does not rise
In glory to amaze all eyes
With heavenly hosts of angels? Where
May Christ be found, more than in me?
He gives Himself that I may live;
To find Him, I need only give
Myself to life and Him, and He
Shall bless and break me as the bread
With which my fellow men are fed.

NOTHING IS ALTOGETHER SEPARATE

Nothing is altogether separate.
There is a pattern in which all things fit;
Where does self end and otherness commence?
Center am I? and not circumference?
I look at the pattern things make and I sense
That nothing occurs that does not occur to me
And all that I do alters totality.
There is a pattern. How can I touch one strand?
The wave I set in motion with my hand
Washes the far shore of an unseen land.
All things distinct and individual
Are patterns in a pattern, and through all
That is I feel a single meaning run;
I look at the many, and I see the One;
Through life's unfinished business, the undone
Deed, the lost dream, the meaningless fact and
        flaw,
I glimpse the perfect beauty of love's law.

REALITY

Seafoam and surf and shooting stars with tails,
Venus and an impalpable moon that pales
And waxes—just such subtle, passing stuff
For God to make His world of is enough.
The Lord of Living has the power to strike
All thoughts from one mind's mold and from one
        seed
Can fill infinity, if there be need,
Yet has not made two moonlight nights alike.
Watching the night go down time's endless track,
I sense that it will nevermore come back,
And everlasting beauty must be caught
Now or will everlastingly be naught.
But I, time's changeling, do not find it strange
Because forever is forever change.
I cannot see or touch the All-in-All,
But listening I can catch His still footfall
This instant on the wind, and I can trace
In this moonlight reflections of His face.
Tonight I stand in darkness on the shore
And cannot clearly see, yet sense the more
Clearly the meaning and reality
Of the one Spirit in all things and me.

ONENESS

Out on a cape where sea and land
Are almost one I like to stand;
There, boundaries become unfixed,
Sea, earth, and I all intermixed.

Or sometimes I am swept along
A crowded street, one with the throng,
And losing consciousness of me
Feel only my humanity.

Or in the silence of a prayer
I find God's presence everywhere,
My heart dissolves in God's one heart—
Where does God end? where do I start?

PRESENCE

Lord, You are everywhere:
In the infolding air;
Embosomed in the globe,
The heavens like a robe
Of splendor round You furled!
The vast voluptuous world
Is but the shadow of
Your unencompassed love.

You are in everything,
Brute, bird, and blossoming.
You lap my limbs with grace;
Your likeness fills my face;
I seek you and I find
You hidden in my mind:
You in my inmost part,
I inmost in Your heart!

I AM MY FATHER'S CHILD

I am my Father's child.
Within, around, above,
Beneath me is His presence
And in my heart His love;
His life is in my body;
His thoughts are in my mind;
And in my world His riches
On every hand I find.

SIZE

How vast a universe! On every side
Crowded with worlds like ours it rushes out
Into a darkness infinitely wide.
Who, looking at the vastness, does not doubt
Man's meaning sometimes, seeing him so small
Beside the flaming swarms of stars and suns?
How can the Lord, having to care for all
This glory, find time for such little ones?
But when I feel dwarfed by the vastness of
The world, I think how He, whose throne is space
And footstool is the stars, is also love
And of my heart has made His dwelling place.
How little God must have regard for size
Who looks upon us with a Father's eyes!

SEARCH

I sought Him, oh, I sought Him night and day;
I prayed and prayed; I knelt and cried aloud;
I whipped myself for sins that kept away
The Lord I loved; I praised Him and I vowed
Alms to the poor and tithes to Him; I kept
Long silences and played the deaf-and-dumb;
I counted beads of blessings and I wept
Beads of despair—and still He did not come.

Yet all the time He filled the earth and sky;
Through every truth I learned He spoke His
          thought;
In every man I met He passed me by;
With my mind thought His thoughts, with my
          hands wrought
His works—but I was blind and could not see
Him who was my own heart in search of Me.

REVELATION

"Give me a revelation, Lord!"
The young man cried in despair.
Spring bloomed, and he rejoiced to see
Spring's beauty everywhere,
Spring green on every bush, spring birds,
Spring flowers in the air.

But, "Give me a revelation, Lord!"
He cried. Love filled his life
And blessed him with good pleasant friends
And a fair, gentle wife
And a gift to lift men's hearts and bring
Peace to their inward strife.

But, "Give me a revelation, Lord!"
He cried. He strove to do
As well as he knew how the work
That he was fitted to,
And to what truth he thought he saw
He labored to be true.

But, "Give me a revelation, Lord!"
Still constantly he cried.
How often must the Lord have wished
To draw the youth aside
And whisper gently in his ear,
"Dear child, how I have tried!"

YOU DO NOT HAVE TO GO TO GALILEE

If you would find your Lord, you need no chart,
You do not have to go to Galilee;
But you need ears to hear and eyes to see
And most of all you need a loving heart.
Go half-a-globe away—still you will find
Him not among the fields where once He stood,
But only in your acts of brotherhood.
Would you seek out the Lord of love? Be kind!
Then He who said to men, "Love one another,"
May softly come and call you, "Little brother!"

NOT BY MIGHT

How few the things that can be done by might!
High aims are thwarted by excess of will;
Only when thought is free can mind take flight.
I do not have to press, but to be still.
I fish, but it is God who fills the net;
I dig, but it is God who fills the well;
Life is not mine to order but to let
Its living power flow through me and impel
Me forward. Would I grasp infinity?
I cannot by hard striving reach the goal,
But I can let the Infinite use me
And know my instant oneness with the whole.
I cannot find You, God, by seeking far,
But I am quiet—and there, God, You are!

PERFECTION'S IMMINENCE

I have gone down a road and had a sense
Suddenly of perfection's imminence.
The same leaves trembled in the sunlight, still
It was as if I had come round a hill
And looked for the first time at reality.
Men live on the edge of a world they never see,
But sometimes I have drawn aside the screen
And felt through to the real and serene
Beyond the world of forms whose shadows pass
Across my mind as in a looking glass.
Then I have been as in another land;
I have stood upon the verge of beauty and
Felt a reality too beautiful to bear
About to reveal itself through the electric air.

THE WHEEL TURNS

The wheel turns—you and I
Turn with it like the sky,
Like time that makes its swing
From spring around to spring.
No one can surely say
He knows the why or way
In which this whirling world
Through whirling gulfs is hurled.
But when I seek the real
In thought or prayer, I feel
Often a sense serene—
Life's meaning is not mean.
Out to the farthest star,
We live and move and are
A Mind's divine excess;
Of no mean, meaningless
Pattern are we a part,
But pulses in a Heart.

LOVE'S BLOSSOMING

God must love happiness,
For He made flowers—
As if from an excess
Of happy powers!

For flowers are love's own warm
Embodiment—
Here perfume has a form
And light a scent;

Flowers are fragilities
And rainbows of
Fragrance. To have made these,
God must be Love,

And love the world He wrought—
For there to spring
Into His mind the thought
Of blossoming.

FOOTPRINTS

Footprints—
In the new snow
I follow them.

God, too, makes footprints—
Across nothingness.

Sunrise and sunset,
Day and night,
The earth and sun and stars,
Flowers of spring,
Summer harvests,
Autumn leaves,
Winter snow—
These are His footprints.

Order and beauty and growth,
Healing for the body,
New thoughts for the mind,
Peace for the spirit—
I see where He has been.

And in me,
I trace His footprints
By my aspirations.

Lord, Lord,
Make my life
Your footprint.

TRANSFORMATION

In the invisible God's tireless hand
Fashions the wonder that at last appears,
Transmuting the dull stuff of circumstance
Into the rainbow shimmer of romance;
And he that can sees pearls in grains of sand,
Diamonds in coal, fresh poems in stale tears.

The ugly duckling, hoping it would die,
Had never dreamed it might become a swan;
The worm all humbly goes and never knows
That one day it will be a butterfly;
The night does not anticipate the dawn;
The thorn has no foreknowledge of the rose.

Who has the faith and foresight to surmise
What mighty unseen changes life has wrought?
Out of the chrysalis of our defeat
Bursts greater glory than we ever thought,
And he who does not blindly shut his eyes
May find a rainbow in a muddy street!

THE RAINBOW

God's shadow is the rainbow. When He stands
Upon the clouds and brings an end to storm,
And stills the sky, a sparrow in His hands,
The sun shines through Him and reveals His form,

The shimmering sum of all the lights we know,
The rainbow; and before it fades away,
All men who can look up to catch the glow.
The shadows that we cast are always gray,

But not the shadow of Infinity.
The rainbow is a fair and perfect round,
But half of it is all we ever see.
I wonder if the rest goes underground

And then in spring appears to us again
In the bright colors flowers are fashioned of,
The many-colored flowers that show to men
The rainbow of His shadow, who is Love.

THE FRUIT OF GOD

I would I might become the human tree
Of God and give with no thought to withhold
From life whatever gifts I have in me;
The fruit of God is better than fine gold.
I plant my thought-trees in the field of mind,
Trees of imagination, tres of reason,
But would not have them bear after their kind;
I would have them bear God's fruit in His own
        season.
For sometimes there appears upon the bough
A harvest no man had foreknowledge of,
A fruit no tongue has tasted until now,
The golden apples of God's perfect love.
I would not give out of what I possess
But out of God's exuberance and excess.

WHITE BIRCHES IN WHITE SNOW

White birches in white snow
Underneath white clouds show
How white is always white,
But with it God can write
And never twice the same
Way sign His secret name.

God must, I think, express
Himself through me no less
Than snow or birches. He
Will write His name through me
And in a way no one
Before has ever done.

MAY CANTICLE

Now sunlight's seamless robe
Enwraps the glowing globe
In holiday attire.
The world becomes a choir:
The budding woods are green
Hymns; even the unseen
Air, light-suffused and calm,
Rolls round us like a psalm.
And shall my mind not be
As much as bird or tree
A canticle of praise?
Do I too not have May's
Delight in livingness
And shall I laud God less
Than flowers that pour their notes
From fragrant meadow throats?
The Lord of love and spring
And joy-in-life I sing.

MY SOUL'S THANKSGIVING

Praise God, my soul and all that is in me!
Praise Him, my acts and dreams! Praise Him, my
      reach
Of spirit! Pour His praises out, my speech,
In words! My silence, praise Him silently!
My dexterous hands, deft artificers of
Fair forms, contrive Him praises! Singing blood,
Leap in my pulses joyously, a flood
Of praise! And heart that He has made for love,
Repeat your love of Him! Soar, soar, my thought,
Praise Him by aiming high yet keeping touch
With sense! And senses, by enjoying much
The world of loveliness His love has wrought,
Praise Him! My prayers and my abundant living,
Silence and speech, affirm my soul's thanksgiving!

EASTER

Sun, sing the risen Lord with tongues of fire
    In psalms of light and anthems of the morning;
Roots underground, press higher and press higher,
    Make a green miracle for His adorning;
Bare boughs, leaf forth, bear beauty everywhere
    Till like a bride before Him earth rejoices;
Sweet birds, in faith dance on the dancing air,
    Choir Him, in jubilee lift up your voices;
Leap, lambs, for love on the upleaping hills;
    Freshets of spring, run like a hymn before us;
Blow, blow your golden trumpets, daffodils,
    Shout glory like a hallelujah chorus;
Imprisoned butterflies, put forth your wings;
    Snakes, molt your skin; frogs, free from winter's
        prison,
Praise Him in unknown tongues; wild newborn
        things,
    Coney and fawn, fear not—is He not risen?

Is He not risen, heart, in cloud and clod?
    In flower and flood? How can you doubt Him,
        seeing
Here, everywhere the resurrected God?
    Heart, He is risen inmost in your being!

WISDOM

The wise and learned sage
On the pretentious page
Writes: "In two words defined,
God is divine mind."

But infants' helpless wiles,
Mere cockleshells of smiles,
Say without words or art,
"God is the human heart."

CHRISTMAS TRUTH

What tale is lovelier or stranger
Than that of God's birth in a manger!
Had I on that first Christmas Eve
Been sent to find Him, I believe
I would have sought in the temple or
Gone knocking at the palace door;
To think to look in a stable yard
To find my God would have been hard.

But if God may be found in a stable stall,
I may not be too mean or small
To give Him birth. I may in me
Discover a divinity.
To find God in the least of things—
This is the hope that Christmas brings.
Christ from His manger cries to the lowly
The truth that every man is holy.

GOD SEES THAT WE ARE GROWING

We are all children, large or small,
Some young, some older, that is all.
God, I am sure, does not expect
Children to always be correct.
This earth is but a little star
And we its human creatures are
Not often brave or wise or strong
Or true to what is best for long.
Yet through our clouds of dark unknowing,
I think God sees that we are growing;
He sees us stumble, sees us err,
But sees we are not what we were.
And when we turn from love and run
Away from truth, He does not shun
Us then, but loves us all the more—
Is this not what a God is for?
Children, you are the offspring of
Our Mother Life, our Father Love.

HIS!

All men are branches of
The vine that is God's love;
The frailest outthrust shoot
Is nurtured by this root.

We grow upon one vine.
What then shall I call mine?
Of everything that is,
What shall I say but "His!"

THE HEART OF ALL

Thank You, Lord, that I am part
Of a world that has You at its heart.
Though world and I may wander far
From truth and peace—lost child, lost star!—
Wherever in the dark we turn
There, at the heart, Your kind eyes burn;
There in the stillness Your footfall;
There in the night of space, in all
That is, your face! Lo here, lo there,
Christ in the heart of everywhere—
Whether I run or I stand still,
Wherever I am, God's holy hill!
At the heart of things, in the heart of me,
Patient love abidingly.

I AM THERE

Do you need Me?

I am there.

You cannot see Me, yet I am the light you see by.

You cannot hear Me, yet I speak through your voice.

You cannot feel Me, yet I am the power at work in your hands.

I am at work, though you do not understand My ways.

I am at work, though you do not recognize My works.

I am not strange visions. I am not mysteries.

Only in absolute stillness, beyond self, can you know Me as I am, and then but as a feeling and a faith.

Yet I am there. Yet I hear. Yet I answer.

When you need Me, I am there.

Even if you deny Me, I am there.

Even when you feel most alone, I am there.

Even in your fears, I am there.

Even in your pain, I am there.

I am there when you pray and when you do not pray.

I am in you, and you are in Me.

Only in your mind can you feel separate from Me, for only in your mind are the mists of "yours" and "mine."

Yet only with your mind can you know Me and experience Me.

Empty your heart of empty fears.

When you get yourself out of the way, I am there.

You can of yourself do nothing, but I can do all. And I am in all.

Though you may not see the good, good is there, for I am there.

I am there because I have to be, because I am.

Only in Me does the world have meaning; only out of Me does the world take form; only because of Me does the world go forward.

I am the law on which the movement of the stars and the growth of living cells are founded.

I am the love that is the law's fulfilling.

I am assurance.

I am peace.

I am oneness.

I am the law that you can live by.

I am the love that you can cling to.

I am your assurance.

I am your peace.

I am one with you.

I am.

Though you fail to find Me, I do not fail you.

Though your faith in Me is unsure, My faith in you never wavers, because I know you, because I love you.

Beloved, I am there.

LIFE IS A WONDER

Weigh the world and pry asunder
All things to their inmost core,
You will find them made of wonder;
Everything is something more.

Life is wonderfully strange
And strangely wonderful, I find,
Being mostly made of change
And the magic stuff of mind.

Even wonder has not caught
All that we are meant to be;
God made us out of His best thought
Thinking of infinity.

IF THOUGHTS HAD SHAPES

If thoughts had shapes like things,
I wonder what they'd be—
Would wonder not be wings
And reverie a sea?

If hope looked like a seed,
Would lilies grow for grace,
Would worry be a weed,
Despair a barren space?

Would thoughts of truth not find
A rainbow's radiant form,
And would not peace of mind
Be sunlight after storm?

And love, what shape would show
Love patient, warm, and true?
All you I love, I know
That love would look like you.

DIVISION

How much of what I see,
So tangible and fair
Of form, is really there
And how much is in me?
Which is thought? which is thing?
I look at earth and find
A world as fair as mind,
Bright as imagining,
Real as a reverie.
What shall divide the stream
And separate the dream
From the reality?
When I look at the sky
Sometimes I find it hard
To tell which one is starred,
The depths of space or I?

MOONLIGHT IS NOT TO SEE BY

Moonlight is not to see by, but to feel
Not actuality, but how unreal
All real things are. No more than clouds or dreams,
Moonlight's half-world is not, but only seems
To be; the moon-spell, forceless, formless, wan
As water changes all it falls upon.
Upon the bottom of the sea of night
Among the watery meadows of moonlight
There lies a fox-fire, glow-worm sort of world;
Its fields are nebulous, its air is pearled,
Even its walls are only shadows cast
By shadows and like shadows will not last.
Still the world has a luminous, clear look
As if it were a drawing in a book
Of old love tales that never did occur
To folk that never lived in times that never were.
But in an hour or two the spell will pass
And day will melt the moon-frost on the grass.

THINK VIOLETS

Violets do not bloom till April here
Or even May, come years when spring is slow,
But I can have them any time of year
Merely by thinking violets. And lo,
There they are in a moment in my mind,
Small, shy, wild, gentle blossoms winking out
From heart-shaped leaves, as fair as I could find
If later I should search for miles about.
Just for the trouble of imagining,
Violets in March, the sweet fragility
Of fragrance, O the very breath of spring!
And in imagination I am free
To take as many blossoms as I care
To pick, yet always find as many there.

A BEAUTY ON THE LAND

There lies a beauty on the land,
But it is hard to understand
What is the glory in the sky
And on the stranger passing by.
The small sun does not rise or set;
The pavement glistens onyx-wet;
The little lights shine here and there;
A winter damp is in the air.
Yet all the gray familiar places,
All the streets and all the faces,
Wear a look of faraway.
It is an ordinary day,
Yet everywhere I look I find
A beauty that I passed by blind
An hour ago. Sometimes I think
We spend our life on beauty's brink,
And never open up our eyes
To see how warm, how close it lies.

SUNRISE

Sunrise is never sudden but comes slowly.
Out of His heaven-bowl God pours His holy
Water of clear and crystal light to run
Through the rose window of His perfect sun
And fall into our mind. In the beginning
We sense not light so much as darkness thinning;
Dawn touches first the tips and tops of things—
The mind to catch the morning must have wings,
And when the day is cloudy, day may start
Not so much in the sky as in our heart.
Yet after a while, all imperceptibly,
We rise and look around us—and we see!

SEA-STUFF

I live in an electric sea
That flashes in and over me.
Electric is the solid ground—
Its particles like bubbles bound;
Electric the transparent air—
Rivers of fire flow everywhere,
Too vast, too luminous for sight.
Heaven and earth are only light,
The momentary shape of motion,
A dazzling, dancing, living ocean.
Heaven and earth are not enough—
I am myself this strange sea-stuff.

TO THINE OWN SELF

The lake looked at the mountain, and thought,
"O fortunate mountain, rising so high,
while I must lie so low.
You look far out across the world
and take part in many interesting happenings,
while I can only lie still.
How I wish I were a mountain!"

The mountain looked at the lake, and thought,
"O fortunate lake, lying so close
to the warm-breasted earth,
while I loom here
craggy, cold, and uncomfortable.
You are always so peaceful,
while I am constantly having to battle
howling storm and blazing sun.
How I wish I were a lake!"

All the time, quietly,
the mountain was coming down
in silver streams to run into the lake,
and the lake was rising as silver mists
to fall as snow upon the mountain.

RIVERS HARDLY EVER

Rivers hardly ever run in a straight line.
Rivers are willing to take ten thousand meanders
And enjoy every one
And grow from every one—
When they leave a meander
They are always more
Than when they entered it.
When rivers meet an obstacle,
They do not try to run over it;
They merely go around—
But they always get to the other side.
Rivers accept things as they are,
Conform to the shape they find the world in—
Yet nothing changes things more than rivers;
Rivers move even mountains into the sea.
Rivers hardly ever are in a hurry—
Yet is there anything more likely
To reach the point it sets out for
Than a river?

AND NOT A SOUND WAS HEARD

I sat and looked at the mountain and I laughed.
I laughed not because the mountain was there
but because I was there.
I laughed to be alive—
and what am I alive for if not to laugh?

I said to the mountain,
"I believe I have the right to address you, sir.
Princes can speak to mountains,
and poets are at least the equal of princes."
Then I heard the mountain laughing.
I wondered,
Is this mountain laughing at me or with me?

Suddenly I sensed
that the trees were laughing, too,
and the streams and the grass and the rocks
and the earth under my feet;
we laughed—they and I—
there upon the laughing mountain,
rocking through space together,
rolling with the laughter of being!

IF YOU REACH

The stars crowd close around me when I walk
At night sometimes. Like swarms of summer flies
Circling my head they dance before my eyes,
Would dart into my mouth if I dared talk.
To keep the stars from catching in my hair
I try to brush them from me, but my hands
Get tangled with the light as in the strands
The little spiders spin upon the air.
Some learned people think that stars are far
Away, but they seem close to me as sight,
Friendly and warm and near as candlelight;
I feel a kindly kinship with a star.
Light-years are for astronomers, I teach
That you can touch the heavens if you reach.

DEEP CALLETH UNTO DEEP

An edgeless, endless, boundless press
Of water and wind and wind and water,
Sea is an overwhelmingness.
Sea is a meaning hard to utter,
Sea is a sound, a taste, a smell,
A seething on the skin, a yearning,
The lift of the long gray slanting swell,
The tug of the tide, the waves returning,
Withdrawing, churning in unrest,
Shingle and sand, tossed up, hurled under,
Cast forth, drawn back, a foaming zest,
A surge, an everlasting thunder
On sandy beach and rocky shelf,
Shaping itself in waves that batter
Landward and break, shaping itself
In waves that form only to shatter,
Momently calm, momently storm,
Water and wind strange and estranging,
The ever-formless seeking form,
The always changeless changelessly changing.

SINGER

One morning in my tree
A bird sang cheerily;
It did not seem to care
If I stood listening there,
And when its song was through,
Straightway away it flew
And did not bow or pause
To wait for my applause.

REDBIRD

Before the earliest edge of spring
He comes to the empty tree to sing,
Cocksure, cavalier, caroling, crested,
Flash-of-fire winged, burning breasted,
Not like a cardinal, like a king!

The wind is sharp and the boughs are bare.
He does not care—he has an air!
Fortune's favorite, destiny's darling,
Envy of robin, wren, and starling,
Elegant, arrogant, debonair,

Lover and poet nonpareil,
Careless of heaven, safe from hell,
Indifferent to fame and folly,
Never a moment's melancholy,
And a voice like a god, a voice like a bell!

Singer who has not been curbed
By the want of world or word,
Sing, O life-lusting, joy-exalting,
Passionate, perfect, mortal-vaulting,
Flame-colored, heart-colored, heart-flame bird!

MARCH WEED

March green brings spring's first beauty—it is shy—
Some looking here see weeds and turn away.
But I see life, crack-crowding, winter-braving,
With all its wonder, all its flame flags waving,
Hear here its gay triumphing trumpets play!

There's something about green things that starts
                    hearts singing,
Pushing up at the sky,
Pushing through death's debris
Airily, merrily, verily
Life out of death springing!

This is the valor passing duty—
May's pink-white perfect loveliness
Has not this beauty,
This touch to heal and bless:

Flowers are but weeds that know their places,
Flowers are weeds with happy faces.

OH, YES, FOR YOU!

Now small leaves open, small birds sing,
Small streams run full, and it is spring;
The winter melts to its icy core.
Hey, you there, what are you waiting for?
Have you woes so deep and hopes so few
That spring can come back and not for you?

If leaf and stream and bird can tell
When it is spring, you know as well;
You have a green life as much as a tree,
And like a spring freshet your thought can run
          free,
And more than a bird, if you've faith to try,
You can rise in your spirit and sing and fly!

INVISIBLES

O the invisible air
I scarcely know is there!
I cannot feel its press,
It seems but emptiness,
But empty seeming,
Yet it is teeming.

Reality may be
Something we cannot see,
Yet no less real for being
Too clear for seeing.

THE GLEAM OF FAITH

The sun was shining on the hill
Although on every side the rain
Kept falling steadily and chill.
But I looked upward and saw plain
The whole hill glow as if on fire,
Like revelation, like a dream
That bids the dreamer come up higher.
So sometimes through our gloom, a gleam
Of faith comes flashing through the mind,
And though it shortly fades away,
It leaves a brighter world behind,
Fairer by that remembered ray.

APPLE ORCHARD

Orchards are profitable, orderly,
Stretched out in straight lines everywhere you
       look;
But they are lessons in geometry
Not out of Euclid but a fairybook.
Walk here in May, and you may understand
How such neat, gray, close-clipped, domestic things
On each blunt twig may feel life's kindling hand
And suddenly be lifted up on wings!
What low unlovely root could ever guess,
Patiently grubbing in the dark all day,
It labors to produce this loveliness?
Bare boughs! Are you so sure it is not May?
Will your gray heart be shaken with surprise
When beauty blossoms forth that blinds the eyes?

WHAT ARE THE LEAVES?

What are the leaves of trees
But hardened light?
Leaves catch the flight
Of something no one sees
Till it is caught—
Is light sun's thought?
Out of this merest trace,
This nothing, empty space,
Leaves without strength or strife,
Merely content to be
Part of the growing tree,
Form life!

CORN

Corn grows so fast you can hear it grow.
But the sound of growing things is no
Sound for a careless heart to catch;
You need sharp ears and a heart to match,
A heart in tune with life, in love
With the world and all the wonder of
God's things! Then on a summer night
When everything inside is right
And everything outside is still
And your will is one with the one great will,
You lie and listen and you hear,
As much with the mind's as the body's ear,
Shoot and blade and stalk unfold,
Tassel and silk and ear of gold,
And you feel the urge, the urgency
Of life, the welling will to be!
Then in the quietness you know
How passionately God's things grow;
You feel your spirit growing tall,
Reaching to be one with all
Reality! Heart's span by span
Grows up the spiritual man!

NO LONGER IN THE SPRING

This is the end of summer:
Autumn outside the door
Pauses like a latecomer;
Spring's posies are no more
Nor sweet birds' hurly-burly;
Now all things nod and wait;
The hour, though it be early,
Has yet the look of late.
The year is yellowing,
The petaled days are flying—
No longer in the spring
With all the glad birds crying.

HOARFROST FOREST

The hoarfrost forest, glittering, still,
Stood growing by the winter hill;
Ice-crowned, immaculate it stood,
Not growing like a living wood
But like a forest in a spell
Where no bird cried and no leaf fell;
And yet it put forth flowers of pale
Perfection, exquisitely frail,
Frozen fragilities of light.
This was a wood you dreamed by night
Or looked at in a looking glass—
That if you looked away would pass.
And so it was. When later on
You came again, the wood was gone.
Bleak trees rose empty in the air;
The hoarfrost forest was not there.

SNOW-FLOWERS

Now winter's flowers fill the air.
How different from the summer kind
They are, but when the fields lie bare,
They look as lovely, to my mind.

Where are the daisies half so white
As these brief blossoms of the storm?
As fragile, fair, and pure as light,
Almost too beautiful for form.

Summer has flowers, but has none such
As these flung from the wind-tossed bough
Of winter, bitter cold to touch!
And still they warm the heart somehow.

SONG FOR SUNSET

Sun, cry. Air, shout. Clouds, trumpet. Make
A music out of sky. Light, break
Forth into hallelujahs like
A hallelujah choir. Space, strike
The strings of emptiness. Rejoice,
You heavens. Tongues of flame, give voice
In hymns of fire. As by trombones,
Day, shake the angels on their thrones.

Then, when the singing light
Is muted by the night,
First star—star in the west—
Shine softly, like a rest.

WHAT LIES BEYOND?

Beyond the farthest cape, what lies?
Beyond the islands of surmise,
The shallow waters where we ply
Our lives, beyond the reach of eye
Or even thought, what lies out there?
Sometimes I stand for hours and stare
Out, out beyond imagining.
The waves that break around me bring
Only a sense of more, yet more.
I think there is no farthest shore.
O God, where shall the limits be?
Your pattern is infinity.

TO SOAR

A will in me
won't settle for
less than the more
I ought to be.

I feel it strain
against the tug
of the tether, hug
of the downward rein.

Each particle
throughout my whole
being, body and soul,
feels the mystic pull

to be more than I
have dreamed I might
be, child of light
and the Most High.

MY FATHER'S CHILD

I was my father's child;
Now I am taller than
My father. Lank and lithe,
I have become a man.

Yet still the world is wide
And still the sky is high,
And sometimes still inside
Most like a child am I!

And grope for the strong hand
Of wisdom in my doubt,
Hide in the heart of love,
Fear lest it shut me out.

Yet I need only cry,
"Father!" and He is here.
I am my Father's child—
What have I then to fear?

AND BEAUTY, TOO!

Flowers are so beautiful—I see
No reason why they have to be;
Considered practically, would
Not ugly flowers have been as good?
But something more than good enough
Is elemental in the stuff
Of things, a joyous, upward twist
That draws a rainbow from a mist;
That gives a lizard feathered wings
And makes of it a bird that sings;
That chooses an unlikely beast,
Not swift or strong—one of the least—
And calls forth in it man who may
Climb clear to Christlikeness some day!

FAR JOURNEY

Around the globe I have not traveled much,
But in my mind what places I have been:
At all the happy islands of nonesuch
The ships that sail my seas of thought put in.
Sojourning as upon another star
In cities that were never made of stone,
I stay at home and still I journey far
With good companions though I am alone;
I may, down roads found nowhere else but dreams,
Become a wanderer in wondershire,
Or fly hope's fabrications and high schemes
Out to the dim horizons of desire.
Whatever you encounter on your flights,
Moonvoyagers, I have seen stranger sights.

THE ISLANDS

The islands of contentment! Where
Are they that I may journey there?
O mariner, where is the chart
That lists the countries of the heart?
Where may I buy a map of mind?
Of these fair islands I can find
No outlines in a travel-book
Or on a globe. Where shall I look
To learn my own geography?
For this I need a map of me.
The islands of contentment lie
Under no far-off foreign sky;
It is myself I must explore
If I would reach their shining shore.

EXPLORER

There is a world as strange and wide
Within me as the world outside.
What compass can the mind invent
To guide me through the continent
That is myself? The vast unspanned
Seas of forgetting guard that land,
A wilderness, thought-girt, dream-shored,
Unknown, uncharted, unexplored.

Hoping to find in the untracked
Jungle of self footprints of fact
To take heart from and follow through
The undergrowth of false and true,
I set forth and must go alone
To make this unknown land my own.

SIGNPOST

I thought a new thought only yesterday.
Today I came upon it in a book
Out of a mind two thousand years away,
And learned that long ago another took

The way that I take now across the dark,
Seeking the good, the beautiful, the true,
And having reached this same place left a mark
To let me know that he had been here too.

On the night path of life, uncertain where
I am or where the way may lie, I see
Suddenly far ahead a struck match flare
Out of the dark as from eternity;

My heart leaps up and I press on again,
Alone but comraded by unseen men.

JOY IS IN JOURNEYING

Roads are for roaming more
Than for arriving,
As life is mainly for
Being alive in.

Joy is in journeying,
Not journey's ending;
Ways are for wayfaring,
Ways are to wend in.

LIGHT IN THE FOREST

This world so dark and wide
That looms on every side
And looks so like a wood
Is God's, and it is good.
If you have lost your way,
You must take time to pray
And just by being still
You come out on a hill
Where for an instant you
May catch a wider view.

Peace must be something more
Than just an end to war;
It is a discipline
You put on from within.
There is no reign of love
That comes down from above;
God's love must always start
In someone's human heart.

THERE IS A CITY

There is a city on a hill,
I see it as if far away;
I have not come there, but I will,
For I have sought it night and day.

A city no more built by hands
Than heaven's stars or meadow flowers
Or human dreams, and yet it stands
Vaulting, like banners its bright towers.

Where is the city on the hill?
I seem forever on the brink
Of finding it; some day I will—
That hill is in my heart, I think.

THE JOURNEY OF TODAY

Dawn is the threshold of today.
Dawn is an open door
That sends you up a sunlit way
You have not climbed before.
But you can know God does not give
You hills too hard to climb;
His love ordains that you shall live
But one day at a time.
Let go dead yesterday's regret,
Tomorrow's phantom fear;
Live in the living now and let
The present good appear.
Even a stay-at-home must make
The journey of today;
Go with a willing heart and take
Love's lamp to light your way;
Prayer be the staff you lean upon;
With faith your feet be shod.
Today you do not walk alone—
Today you walk with God.

TRUMPET IN MY HEART

I hear a trumpet in my heart
That will not let me rest or stay;
It calls and I must rise and start
Like hound to hollo on my way.

It is a summons never caught
By earthy ears; it is the sound
Of all that men have ever sought
And suffered for and never found.

And I have followed it through pain
And joy and change since I was born,
Hearing forever winding plain
Truth's faint far music like a horn.

BEYOND THE HILLS

Truth is a distant mountain range
Beyond the little hills of change,
Its summits lost in clouds of doubt;
And only he can make truth out
Who dares the perilous ascent
Out of the valley of content.

ALTHOUGH THE CROWD

Although the crowd stood up to cheer
The leap by which you cleared the bar,
The leap by which you failed to clear
May measure what you truly are.

At fortune's lowest ebb a man
May be the closest to the crest;
The race in which he also ran
May be the one he ran the best.

AIM

The runner who has always won
And never staggered to defeat
Has only half learned how to run;
His victory is incomplete
Who never knew the dust and shame
Of failure, straining in the dark!
He only had too low an aim
Who has not ever missed the mark.

TRUSTING AS I GO

Man fences in his mind
Not to shut in but out—
He likes his world defined,
And feels at ease about
The things that have a rim
That was designed by him.

The world is too immense
To take the measure of
And put inside a fence,
Unless the fence be love—
And so I find I must
Accept most things on trust.

But trusting as I go
That things are mainly good
Somehow, I'm sure I grow
More than I think I would
If I could always see
Where boundaries had to be.

CROCUS

I wonder if a crocus
Wishes to come out;
I think it must, like you and me,
Have many times of doubt.

And draw inside its dreary bulb
And peering at the snow
That fills the wide and wintry world
Mistrust its power to grow.

Yet once it takes its heart in hand
And steps into the cold,
It finds itself clothed like a king
In purple robes and gold.

CHANGE

I have resisted change with all my will,
Cried out to life, "Pass by and leave me still."
But I have found as I have trudged time's track
That all my wishing will not hold life back.
All finite things must go their finite way;
I cannot bid the merest moment, "Stay."
So finding that I have no power to change
Change, I have changed myself. And this is strange,
But I have found out when I let change come,
The very change that I was fleeing from
Has often held the good I had prayed for,
And I was not the less for change, but more.
Once I accepted life and was not loath
To change, I found change was the seed of growth.

EVOLUTION

I had a vision and I saw him rise
And lift his huge paws upward at the skies
And claw the air and sway and strain to stay
Erect. There was a look about his face,
And what dumb pleading in the great beast eyes,
And every muscle, tendon, nerve intent
To thrust up to the very firmament.
He tottered, twisted, slipped, gave one fierce groan,
And fell with a bone splintering crash, and lay
Stretched out and stunned and impotent and mute.
He is a brute, I thought. He has no grace
To stand. It was not ever meant. And then,
Out of the mud and muck where he lay prone,
Out of the agony of heart and bone,
I saw him, oh, I saw him rise again!

STRENGTH

Who was not threatened, never quailed;
Who was not tempted, never fell;
Who was not tested, never failed.
Go ask not of the quick and well,
But of the ones who agonize,
What wholeness is; the fallen only
Can tell you what it means to rise;
To learn of friendship ask the lonely.
Go ask the ones who broke and ran
What courage is, not those who stood;
None may know less of virtue than
The saint who has been only good.
For those who went beyond their strength
Alone can tell the measure of
The heart's capacities, the length
To which despair may go, or love.

ONE STEP MORE

A hill is not too hard to climb
Taken one step at a time.

One step is not too much to take;
One try is not too much to make.

One step, one try, one song, one smile
Will shortly stretch into a mile.

And everything worthwhile was done
By small steps taken one by one.

To reach the goal you started for,
Take one step more, take one step more!

IT IS NOT THE STREET

It is not the street that bears us up as we walk—
it is faith.
Without faith, who can stand—
let alone walk?
With faith, what road do we not dare take?
Having faith, one walked on water.
Having faith, some walk on air
and circumnavigate the heavens.
Every step a man takes is a venture in uncertainty—
but when we step on faith,
we step as on a rock of reassurance.
We walk as if God had us by the hand,
and our life is a journey into jubilance.
Children, walk on faith.

UPON THIS FLAME

I watched the rocket flight.
I saw men ride
a thundering plume of flame
serenely out of sight.
They rose astride
a million fiery horses yoked in one dancing blaze
till they flew free
of all our slow earth-crawl and weighty ways.
Like a wind the ship's wash came
shaking the earth and me

and then I saw

the first man rubbing firesticks till his straw
glowed and puffed smoke.
I watched how he leaned and blew
till the fire broke
and the flame crept, leapt, soared, roared
not only in the straw but in his eyes.

And then I knew

that the fire by which men rise
and leave old worlds behind
leaps not so much in the pale
straw or the rocket's tail
as in the mind.

Upon this flame man flies.

IT MAY, I THINK, BE PROVED

It may, I think, be proved
That mountains can be moved
By faith more quickly than
Faith by a mountain can.
What great works has man wrought?
Not one but was a thought
First in the mind of one
Who said, "It can be done!"
A man with faith to try
Gave man the wings to fly,
And One with faith to give
Himself to life and live
Made even death retreat.

Man, have you much to meet?
The victories men win
Are faith persisted in.
That thing man can conceive,
That thing man will achieve.
Never lose faith! Believe!

WHAT CAN FEAR DO?

What can fear do to him who has no fears?
Storms cannot keep the river from the sea;
A quiet heart through life's unquiet years
Flows like a river of eternity.
Pain may torment this finity of flesh
And death may turn this quick to quiet dust,
Yet death cannot make love's perfection less,
Pain cannot alter love's unchanging trust
That there is meaning where no meanings show
And purpose though no purposes shine through,
That life and death are but the ebb and flow
Of being toward the beautiful and true.
Having seen faith where only fear should be,
Through doubt I can reach blind for certainty.

LOOK TO THE SEA

Life's beautiful uncertainties
Stretch out before us like a sea's
Uncharted vasts, and we can fare
Life-ward as far as faith can dare.
What unimagined isles of thought
Lie only waiting to be sought?
O mariner, life has no bound;
An unknown world lies all around
Us everywhere. By you alone
Shall the unknown become the known.
Out, out beyond the edge of dreams,
Past all that's sure and all that seems,
The truths yet undiscovered are.
Look to the sea! Dream high! Dream far!

LIFE'S CHILD

When I was a school boy, I confess
My favorite subject was recess,
And still I do not find it hard
To loiter in my heart's schoolyard
Entranced by all the things that are
Such bright adornments of this star.
I pray I shall not ever be
So grownup that the child in me
Will have no wish to run and play
And sing and dance the hours away.
Oh, may I sometimes in my mind
Leap up and leave my cares behind
And live as if I truly were
Life's child and chief inheritor.

LITTLE THINGS

Lord, in the little things, I pray,
The unrecorded, everyday,
Passing events, may I take joy.
May I have always a small-boy
Mind that can give itself to each
Moment and does not have to reach
Forever for what is not there,
But finds contentment anywhere;
For I would have no need of wings
But what the winged moment brings.

How few the triumphs or defeats
That the most noted person meets!
But every moment, thought by thought
And act by act, a life is wrought,
A life is lived—and I would learn
To live each moment in its turn.
Lord, in the little things, I pray,
The little acts of every day,
Let me find joy. Then I shall be
Contented with eternity.

NOW

Tonight I have the sea and moon,
But such a night is hard to keep;
It will have vanished soon, too soon—
And I'll have many nights to sleep.

And so I will not sleep tonight
But wake and listen to the sea
And let the moon's soon fading light
Cast its pale passing spell on me.

For other nights may come as fair,
And even everlasting bliss,
But in eternity nowhere
Except tonight will there be this.

JUBILANT JOURNEY

Where are you going? What is your destination?
Life is for journeying, not to stand and stay.
Life is a highroad. Life is for elation.
Walk through the wide doors, heart, be on your
            way!

Life is unfoldment. Life is a foment
Of thought and act and feeling. Life is for growth.
Life is for forever. Life is for the moment.
Life is for living. Heart, be not loath

For the jubilant journey! Give yourself to living.
Life is for discovery. Life is always new,
Not for the having and holding, but for giving.
Give yourself to life, and life will give itself to you!

SAILOR

By ways I never charted
And hardly wished to go,
I have sailed an unknown course
On a sea too wide to know.

I have drifted lost at times,
Not sure where the shore might be;
I have searched through storm-tossed nights
For a light I could not see.

But a Higher Wisdom than my own
Has had me in its hand,
And I shall trust that it will bring
Me safe at last to land.

MATRICULATION

School is not a building
but an expanding state of mind.
My schoolhouse has no walls
except the limits of my will to learn.

Everything delivers learned lectures
when I pay attention;
there is no object or event
that does not turn into a textbook
when I study it.

I have gone to school all my life.
When I graduate,
I have no doubt,
God has post-graduate courses
I can enroll in.

KEEPSAKES

After awhile one finds time runs together.
Did it happen last night, last week, last year, ten
Years ago, fifty years ago, or when?
After awhile one comes to wonder whether

It ever happened; some things only seem.
Time is more anesthesia than wings;
And most remarkable of all, the things
That were most real become most like a dream.

Beginning, ending are not far apart.
A life is not a ribbon to unwind;
The knots one tried to tie in the string of the mind
Always at last get tangled in the heart.

Life is a drawer of keepsakes—violets,
A faded photograph—one opens the drawer
And lifts them out to view, but more and more,
Just when they were put in—this one forgets.

WONDERSHIRE

Somewhere a far enchanted country!
A shining land of dream somewhere!
Where lies the land my heart goes hunting?
Have I but dreamt that it is there?

It lies, I think, this side of never
And I will find it one fine day,
For I will look for it forever.
I think I glimpse it far away

At times, past love's and faith's pretending,
Beyond the hills of heart's desire
Where all roads have a happy ending
At last far off in wondershire!

OUT OF FOREVER

A wind from far away, out of forever,
Blows sometimes from I know not what strange
            strand;
Then I am as in a dream, a dream I never
Remember, yet somehow I understand.

I turn, although I know no road returning
To the high country whence my mind's winds
            come
To fill me full of dreams and full of yearning.
What fair land, what far shore the wind blows from

I cannot say, but when the wind is blowing,
It blows to me a sense of truths more true,
Of lives beyond this life, and worlds past knowing.
Companions, does the wind not blow for you?

THANK YOU

Through every sprouting seed
Life without let or heed
Gives, seeking to be more
Than it has been before.

You are a work of love,
The longed-for product of
Perfection's hungering
To form a perfect thing.

All heaven and all earth
Converged around your birth
And labored as you grew
To frame a perfect you!

Printed U.S.A.   1 2 2 F-1 5 M-1 1 -7 3